When the London and North Western Railway Company built the Peterborough branch line in 1845 there were soon many iron ore pits opening up in it's vicinity and connected by this line. In 1854 Duston iron ore pit was opened up commercially and provided regular employment for men in this area for some 60 years. All of the ore was sent away to distant furnaces. I am indebted to the late Mr. William Bailey of Manitoba for allowing me to make available his photographs.

Cover photograph:
"Duston" iron ore engine at Weeden Road depot 1900. Mr W Bailey and Mr Tippleston on the footplate. Mr Bailey Emigrated to Canada after the pits closed in 1909.

£6.99

DUSTON

AND ST. JAMES

A Pictorial History

The Collector and Local Historian

Fred Golby's early life began in Alma Street, St James. He came to live on the new Millway Nurseries in 1947, soon after this, his interest in Local History began, and portrayed here is part of his 50 year long collection of photographs. Since its inauguration, some 25 years ago, he has been a member of the Northamptonshire Industrial Archeological Group.

Acknowledgements

I am indebted to the following for their help in the publication of this book of photographs:
Mr Stafford, Mrs Taylor Mrs Arnold of Northamptonshire Libraries.
Miss Rachel Watson of Northamptonshire Record Office.
The Classic Motor Cycle.
Ordinance Survey (Copyright).
Northampton Mercury.
British Timken.
Circus World Museum.
Bob Whitton, Mr J Bell, Robert Fosset, Mr Faulkner, Mrs J Broome, Canon John Flavell, Kathleen Flavell, Dick Coleman, Mrs Munday, Miss M Young, Miss V Mallard, Mrs J Brown, Mrs Jean Gibbons, Mr Slinn, Mr Jack Downie, Mollie Tomalin, Mr Staughton, Mr M Smith, Mr Andrew North, Miss Bull, Mr. Grimes.

Every effort has been made to trace the original source of the photographs published here and wherever possible gratefully acknowledged.

Published by J. W. F. Golby

ISBN 0 9518569 0 1

Contents

Iron Ore 1

Old Duston and Duston Village 9

Village People 14

Village Stores 18

Village School 20

Duston Church 23

Duston Church Choir 28

Duston Mills 30

Millway 33

British Timken 36

Yarde's Nurseries 38

Nurseries Millway and Mill Lane 43

New Duston Stone 46

Sir Robert Forsetts Circus 50

New Duston 54

Franklins Gardens 61

St James 66

Old Duston, New Duston – 1901

Duston and Old St James – 1898

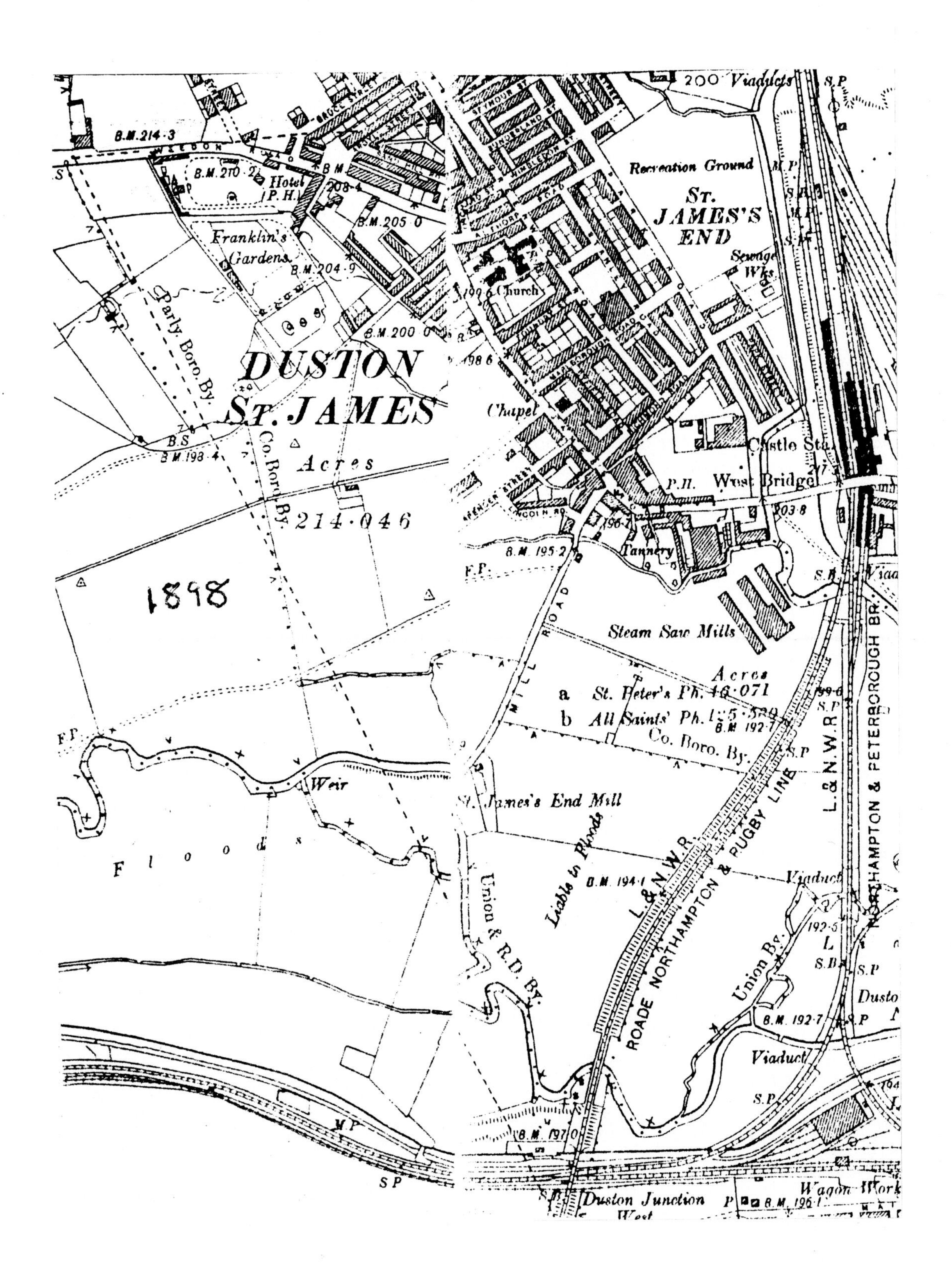

Introduction

This book of photographs records some of the pictorial history of the Parishes of Duston and St James, as collected, largely by Fred Golby of Millway Nurseries, Duston.

Duston, with it's current population of 20,000, is now part of the vast expansion of Northampton, yet in 1845, at the southern end of the Parish, Old Duston village consisted of only 145 dwellings. These dwellings were mostly tied cottages, being part of the estate of some 1,760 acres which was owned for 250 years by the Melbourne family of Derbyshire. At the same time, New Duston was a tiny hamlet at the northern end of the parish, where most of the men worked extracting the famous "Ryland Stone" from stone pits in the Port Road area Meanwhile, from 1845 to 1909, in Old Duston, off the Weedon Road (A45), enormous quantities of iron ore were being extracted. Quarrying is now only carried out on a small scale at New Duston and has been replaced over the years by a variety of industrial, commercial and retail activities.

For centuries approaching the Nene at Westbridge was a tiny hamlet called St James End. St James End Parish was first formed in 1895, as part of the westward expansion of the town of Northampton, from a large area of the Parishes of Dallington and Duston. One side of the St James main road comprised the Dallington land of the then Lord Robert Spencer, including and area as far as the Spencer Bridge Road, whilst the other side, was part of the Duston Parish of Lord Walter Kerr to a point marked approximately by the Red House Public House (now the Red Rover). The early expansion mainly consisted of Boot and Shoe factories surrounded by large areas of workers houses. Latterly the Boot and Shoe industry has declined, apart from the production of specialised quality boots and shoes, to again be replaced by a wide range of alternative employment, ranging from Engineering to retail superstores.

Thus through these photographs dating from approximately the end of the last century to the late 1960's it is hoped that the viewer can appreciate the changing times, in terms of working life, leisure moments, devotional, special occasions and home life. A sequel to this book of photographs will be published later.

Chapter 1 – Iron Ore

Hunsbsury Hill Furnaces Photo (1936) disused for some 15 years, limestone was taken by rail link to these works from Duston when operating fully.

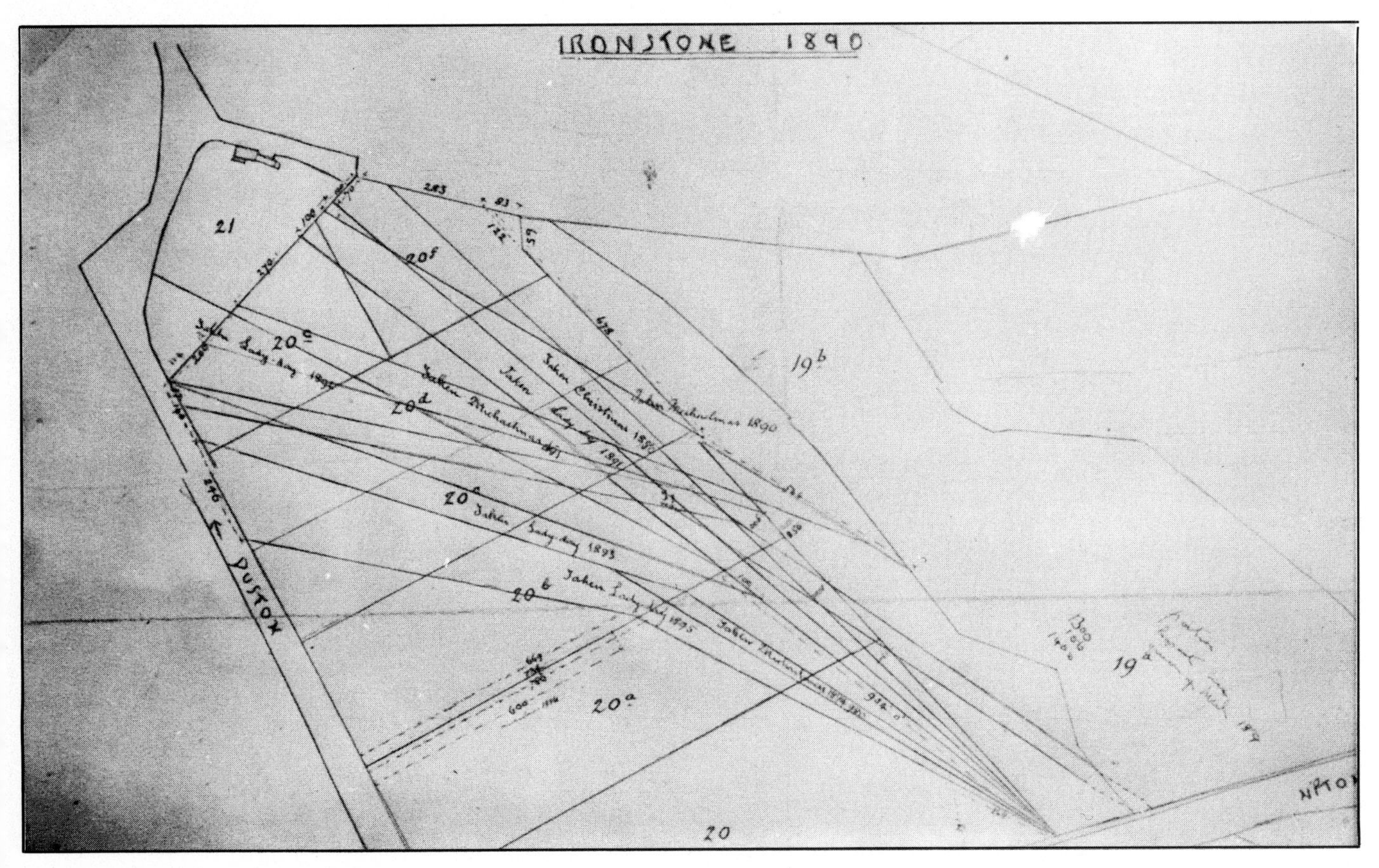

The mineral agent's plan for the extraction of iron ore from Weedon Road to Duston Church in 1890, beginning from number 2 tunnel under the Weedon Road.

Agreement between the Duston Iron Ore Co and
Messrs Whitworth & Co for carriage of traffic between
the St James end coal Wharf & Iron Works and the
Peterborough Branch of the London & North
Western Railway

September 29 1885

The Duston Iron Ore Co agree that they will from
time to time so long as this Agreement
continue convey all the Iron Steel coal and all
articles which the said Messrs Whitworth & Co
may desire to send or convey to or from &
between the said works & coal wharf or yards
to or from the said Railway siding & will
provide sufficient Locomotive power for the
purpose the said Messrs Whitworth providing
proper & sufficient trucks the work to be done
in a proper & business like manner & without
any avoidable delay but so that the conveyance
of such goods sent by or to the said Messrs
Whitworth is not to interfere with the carriage
of the goods and materials of the Duston Iron
Ore Co

Messrs Whitworth & Co agree to keep in repair that
portion of the tramway lying between the said
works and the terminus of the Duston Iron Ore
Co line near the Brickyard and will pay
all rents due upon the land occupied by
that portion of the tramway just named
and also pay all wayleave rents imposed
the said traffic & also keep proper book
of ac at the works shewing all traffic
conveyed & allow copies to be taken and
also will pay [illegible] per ton of 2520 lbs for
all Iron Steel coal or other material

Documents allowing Messrs Whitworth & Co., who owned Stenson Ironworks, permission to use the railroads of the Duston Estate to move their materials on to the London North Westem Railway.

"Peterstone" also at the Weedon Road depot, is was a central store for coal etc. also providing offices and stabling for the many horses used. Good quality bricks were made at the Duston Iron Ore Company brick yard here.

Duston Iron Ore Company's engine sheds now part of Weedon Road Industrial Site, Ross Way in the background (once Brick Yard Lane).

"Duston" leaving the canal bridge before passing over the Blisworth/Peterborough line to the iron ore sidings.

The first Duston Iron Ore pit off Ross Way. Fllled in with refuse during the late 1920's (now industrial site).

Mr Henry Garratt mineral agent for the Duston estate came from the Melbourne estate in Derbyshire, and lived on in Melbourne Lane after the iron ore pits closed.

Iron ore workers beside the enormous Roman limestone tomb found just off Millway (now in Abington Museum).

A Mineral Agent's old house in Melbourne Lane (now demolished).

Wooden viaduct across the flood plane, from the Highlines to the Blisworth canal built in a half circle against the flood tide erected around 1845.

When the Upton Way intersection was built some years ago, huge quantities of in-fill refuse was removed some forty foot deep to begin road foundations, an opportunity to go under number 2 tunnel on the iron ore railroad was reopened, shown on the right hand side of the photo.

Wooden viaduct showing Hunsbury Hill furnaces working in the background.

Duston Irone Ore Company's loco with Duston name plate at company's depot Weedon Road, about 1900.

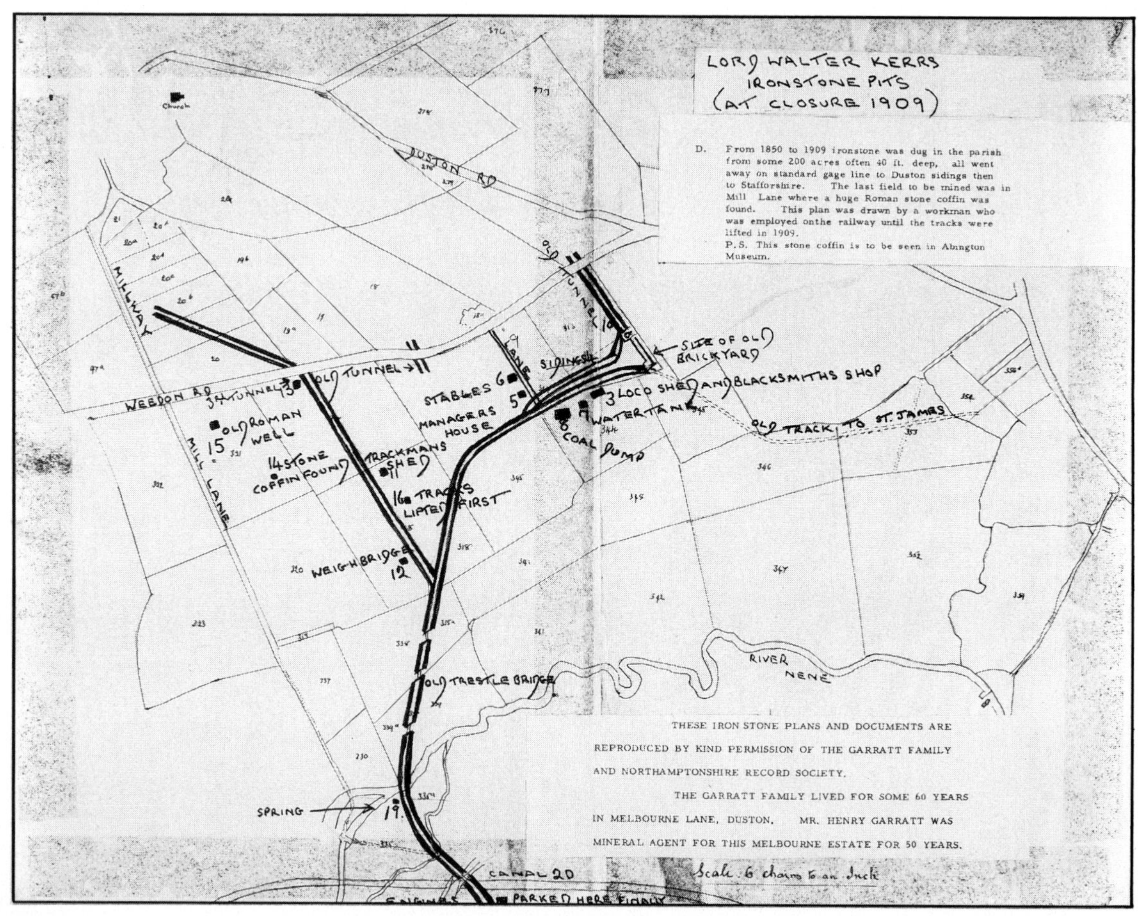

From 1850 to 1909 ironstone was dug in the parish from some 200 acres often 40ft deep, all went away on standard gauge line to Duston Sidings then to Staffordshire. The last field to be mined was in Mill Lane where a huge Roman stone coffin was found. This plan was drawn by a workman who was employed on the railway until the tracks were lifted in 1909 – This stone coffin is to be seen in Albington Museum.

Chapter 2 – Duston Village

Second Lord Melbourne, Melbourne Hall in Derbyshire is now owned by Lord Lothian who's family seat is in Scotland.

Village scene 1880, old cottages on left of picture where now stands chemists shop and post office.

1928
Main Road
with village
lengthman
(roadsweeper)
at work.

The old
cottages in
Chapel Lane,
Main Road.

Sam Harrison's 17th century cottage, before it's demolition it stood at the rear of the village school.

Someone's beloved cottage stood at the end of the small yard opposite the village school at the turn of the century.

Showing Mr Billings house, his grandfather was village builder and undertaker, showing the old yard and buildings on right.

"Oak Lodge" built for Mr Stevenson at the corner of Peverel Road, the renowned Northampton architect who trained under Mathew Holding. Oh! how quiet and peaceful the main road was then!

Samwell's Hatchment, in Upton Church, showing coat of arms with squirrels from where the public house, in Dunston derived it's name.

The Dower house from the west side showing the later Georgian additions and it's Victorian conservatory, the estate drive to Upton House once crossed the Weedon Road to Upton.

Chapter 3 – Village People

Mr and Mrs Bobby Errington who gave land at New Duston for Errington Park

Mr Robert Errington, Mr and Mrs Errington photographed in their pony and trap 1930

Mr and Mrs Jones at Homeleigh Farm 1880

Pantomime 1937 – At village institute by "King's Messengers" church youth organisation, produced by Sid and Doris Reynolds. Sid was instrumental in the early productions of Duston Players at the institute long before the community centre was built. Seated, left to right 2. Peter Cox, 3. Silvia Bass, 4. Geoffery Harison, 7. Mollie Payne, 11. Biddy Goatley. Standing: 2. Jean Scotney, 5. Bernard Harison, 6. Roger Dove, 7. Kathleen Thurley, 8. Joyce York, 9. Jean Thompson, 11. Joan Harrison, 14. Connie Clifton, 16. Geraldine Orland, 17 Muriel Ayers.

The Wilcox family outside their "Rose Cottage" Farm, 1895

Mr Perkins outside
his old cottage in
Chapel Lane

Making hay at
"Highfield",
(now Saxon Rise).
Left right:
Horace Faulkner,
Nell Faulkner,
Jane Faulkner,
Percy Faulkner

1935. Sam Harrison, village lengthman, (road sweeper)

1906. Opening of Duston Village Chapel's new school rooms. This extended building is now used for worship

Hillson's trap, Horace Faulkner and "Spot" the dog

Chapter 4 – Village Stores

Village Stores, 1913, left Percy Faulkner (later became village baker) right Horace Faulkner (later kept the "Melbourne Arms"

Duston Stores showing Pond Farm buildings in 1907, stores were then lit by gas

Duston Stores, 1903 and "Laburnum" Cottage, with Mr Walter Hillson, Bessie Hillson and Miss Jane Faulkner.

Mr Wilcox's coal merchant's cottage, burnt down during the first war next to the bottom shop (opposite the village school), this shop was then Mr Bishop's bakehouse and shop.

Mr Bishop's calendar.

Pond Farm buildings also Timken Hardware Store, 1960.

Chapter 5 – Village School

Top right: 1856, village school from a painting, some 6 or 7 extensions have been added over a hundred years

Bottom Left: The original school still retains it's Main Road frontage.

Bottom Right: Mr Jones, headmaster of Duston village school from 1896 to 1932, he then lived at the school house," Ferndale"

Rose Cottage" Farm (opposite village green) with village school in the backound approximately 1875.

Mr Speight, Headmaster village school 1891. Photographed with his pupils when the population of the village was only 783.

Mr William Bailey's 1890 good attendance certificate presented to him at the village school

The old school master's house (left) during the extensive iron ore excavation in Millway was a public house ('Ihe Wooden Spout)

Chapter 6 – Duston Church

St Luke's Church, Duston. Church Way, 1875, before the church yard was extended westwards in 1898, note the old lamp over the gate, now over the porch door

St Luke's church, seen from Millway, 1880.

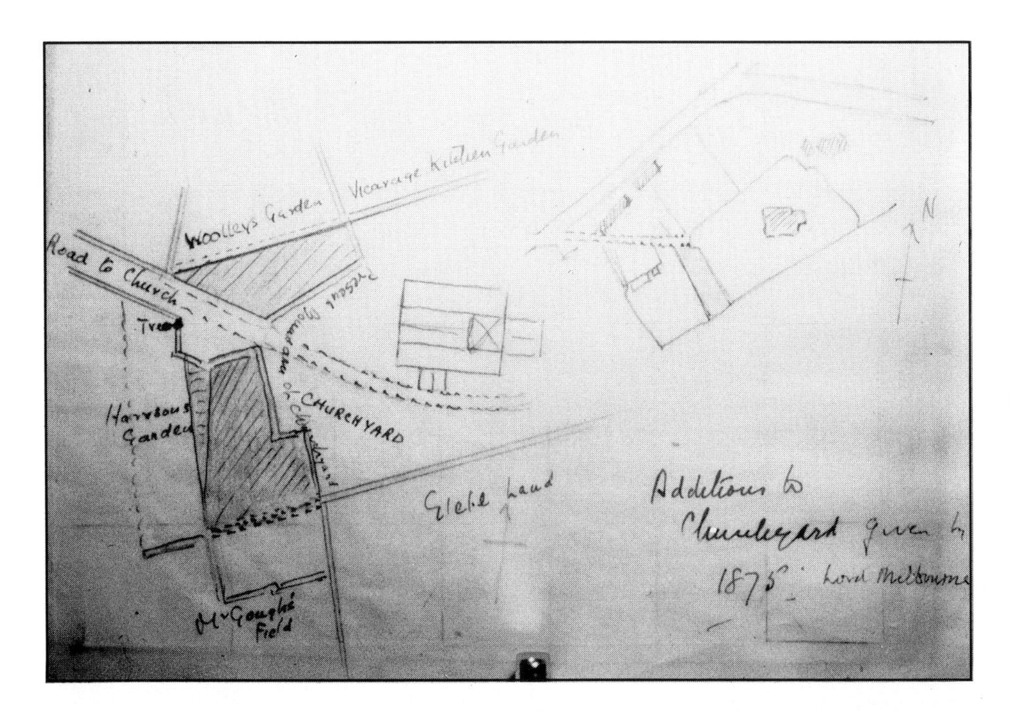

Lord Melbourne's plan for the extension of St Luke's churchyard 1875.

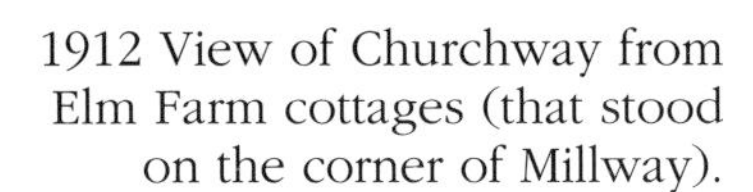

1912 View of Churchway from Elm Farm cottages (that stood on the corner of Millway).

One of four Corbel figures. In the chancel at Duston Church, each representing medieval musicians "Man playing harp".

Witliam Butlin's family tomb in Duston churchyard, this famous iron master lived in Duston House, the huge anchor embedded in granite denoted his association with the Royat Yacht Ctub. He took great interest in the parish and held high office in St Luke's Church, where his Wellingborough works decorative cast iron communion rails can be seen.

Rev. Thompson, vicar of St Luke's Church, Duston, 1935-1942.

The old Duston stone vicarage (now offices) built 1840.

To celebrate Jubilee Day, June 9th, 1935, St Luke's bellringers rang a quarter peal.
Back row left to right Ted Rudkin, Cyril Smith, Jack Clifton, Sid Mundy, Henry Downie.
Front Row:Douglas Shelmerdine, Mr Thompson, Rev. Jones, A R Jones, Tom Bass.

Duston Church bellringers during the incumbency of the Reverend Butcher, 1945,
left to right 1. Tom Bass, 4. Jeff Harrison, 5. Rodger Dove, 6. Sid Munday, 7. Rev. Butcher, 8. Jim Harrison, 9. Henry Downie, 10. Jim Collins, I 1. Geoff Mallard, 12. John Munday, 13. John Ayres.

1930. Bellringers left to right: Cyril Smith, Jack Cliffton, Sidney Munday, Ted Rudkin, Henry Downie, Jack Burgess.

1946 Sunday morning bells at St Luke's Church.

Chapter 7 – Duston Church Choir

1899. Reverend Richardson and Choir. He was the only incumbent to play for the village football team.

1930. St Luke's Church Choir outside the old stone vicarage included are seated: Cecil Payne, Stan Payne, John Wright, Jack Clifton.
Left to right second row: Mrs Jones, Fred Day, Mr Farr, Mr Bailey, The Reverend A R A Jones, Mr Bennett, Dick Wright, Vera Mallard.
Left to right third row: 1. Mr Bcn, 2. Ray Cross, 3. Mr Young, 4. Mr Day, S. Albert Bradbury, 6. Mr Rice, 7. Mr Lawrence, 8. Edna Mallard.
Fourth row: 1. Eileen Harrison, 2. May Harrison, 5. Florrie Cass, 6. Mollie Cabarn.

St Luke's Church Choir during incumbency of the Reverend Butcher. Included are, first row: Jackie Stuart, Sidney McGu nn. Second row: Miss Robrtson, Jill Tomkins, Jeff Harrison. Third row: Donald York, Jeffery Mallard, Joan Palmer, Isla Johnson. Back row: John Favell, Mr Sangster, Mr Robertson, The Reverend Butcher, Rodger Dove.

8th May, 1935. To mark the special occasion of enlarging the village school, shows the bishop of Peterborough leading the procession from St Luke's Church followed by the Reverend Thompson, clergy, choir and congregation.

Section of St Luke's Church Choir, 1962. Back row: Jill Dorricott, Marjorie Cosford, Hazel Bandy, BobBazeley, John Bandy. Jim Allaway. Front row: Michael Reynolds, Andrew Dransfield, Neville Royan, David Allaway, John Golby.

Christmas carols, Duston Church Choir at New Duston, 1959. Left to right Mrs Dobbs, Beverley Dobbs, Mr Dobbs, Jamie Rhodes, Jim Allaway, Gordon Bristow, John Bandy, David Allaway, Marjorie Cosford, Jill Dorricott, Neville Royan

Chapter 8 – Duston Mills

1941, Duston Upper Mill

Duston Upper Mill was working until the estate sale of 1919.

When Northampton Development Corporation acquired Duston Mill the property was declared unsafe, Mr Morris, MP, Reverand Appleton and Mr F Golby met to consider the possibility of saving the property.

Mr Fosdyke who worked most of his life on the River Nene lived at the old Duston Mill House until it was demolished in 1970.

The Upper Nene flood plane around Duston Mill 1932, Duston men who worked at Hunsbury Hill Furnaces before it's closure in 1922 had to walk to Northampton then via Rothersthorpe Road to get to work in winter.

Demolition of Duston Upper Mill.

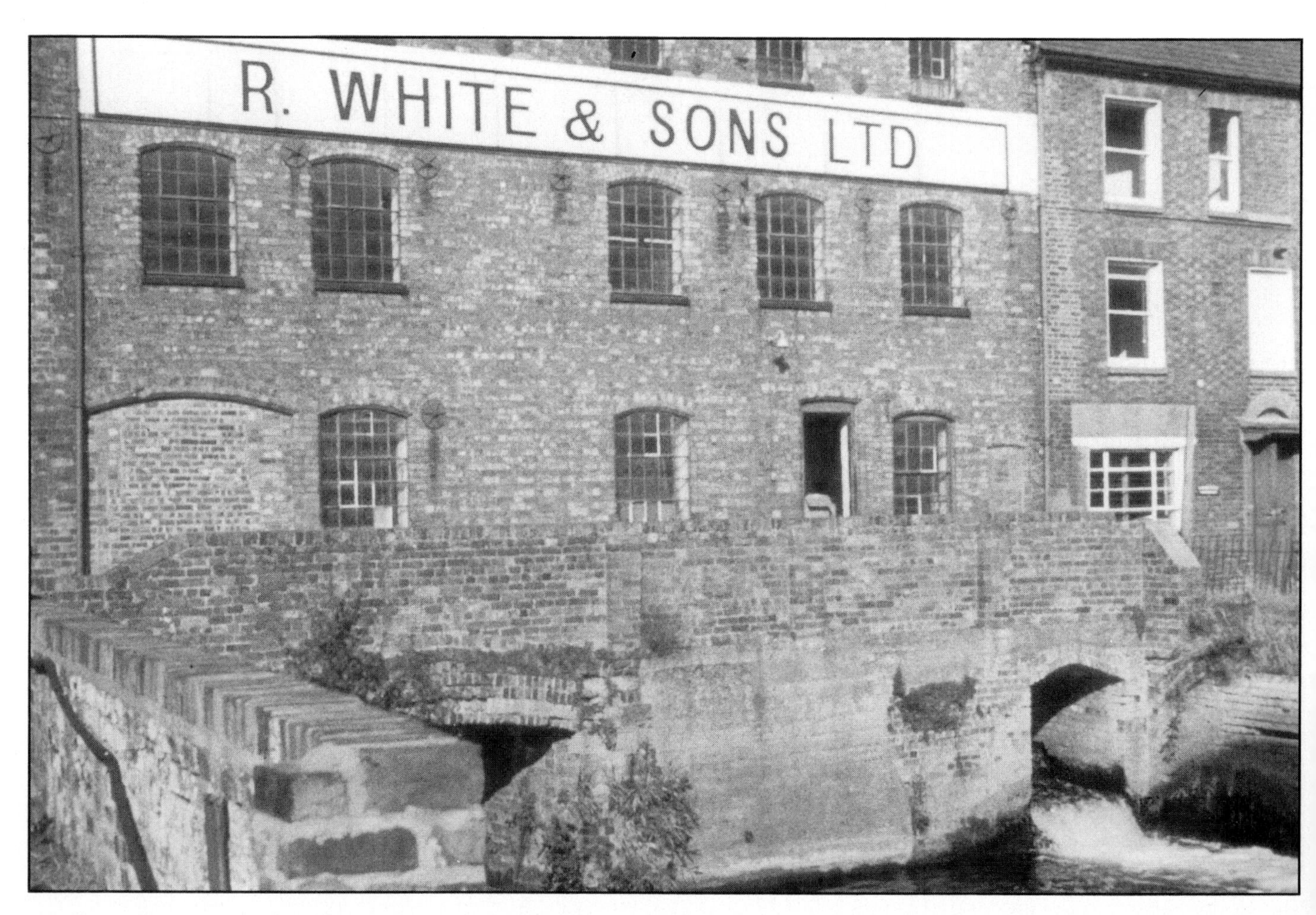

St James Mill (Duston lower mill), was worked until the last war by the Beesley family. This is now part of an industrial site.

Chapter 9 – Millway

1860. Quiet Millway, for children to play (note the tall Elms).

This Millway cottage was burnt down in 1977.

Elm Farm looking west towards Millway from St Luke's Church Tower.

Home from the iron ore pits, Dave Billingham his wife Pheobe in the doorway.

Millway, 1898, neighbours talking in a quiet lane.

Going to school, Millway 1881 towards Elm's Farm.

Chapter 10 – British Timken

First British Timken Show, 1947, in factory fields.

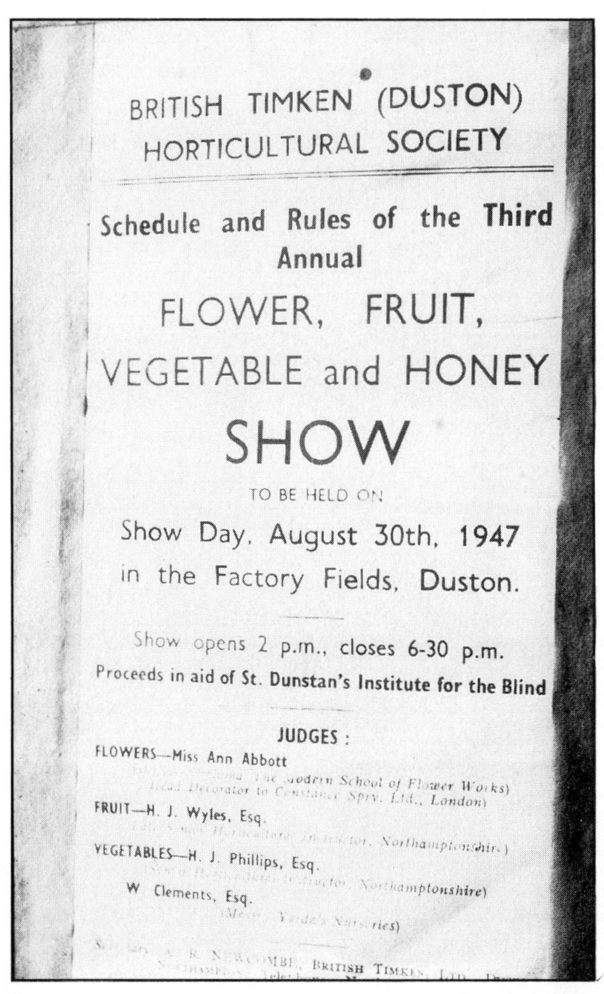

BRITISH TIMKEN (DUSTON)
HORTICULTURAL SOCIETY

Schedule and Rules of the Third Annual

FLOWER, FRUIT, VEGETABLE and HONEY

SHOW

TO BE HELD ON

Show Day, August 30th, 1947
in the Factory Fields, Duston.

Show opens 2 p.m., closes 6-30 p.m.
Proceeds in aid of St. Dunstan's Institute for the Blind

JUDGES :

FLOWERS—Miss Ann Abbott
([illegible] Modern School of Flower Works)
(Head Decorator to Constance Spry, Ltd., London)

FRUIT—H. J. Wyles, Esq.
([illegible] Horticultural [illegible], Northamptonshire)

VEGETABLES—H. J. Phillips, Esq.
([illegible] Instructor, Northamptonshire)

W. Clements, Esq.
([illegible] Nurseries)

[illegible] R. NEWCOMBE, BRITISH TIMKEN, LTD. [illegible]

Schedule of 1947 British Timken Show began on a very small scale but eventuaully grew into one of the outstanding horticultural shows in the country.

Cricket at British Timken, 1950,.

Spectators:
Mr S. Eyles,
Mrs Dove,
Mrs Cosford.

Inside British Timken Horticultural Show marquee, trade and amateur exhibits came from all over the country.

Tea Ladies at British Timken Show, 1947,

Chapter 11 – Yarde's Nurseries

Sam Yarde, Mayor of Northampton 1913, he came to live in the town from Ilminster, Somerset in 1881, soon became involved in town affairs and served many years as town councilor. Based in Abington Square opposite Bradlaugh's statue, this large firm had 7 florist shops in and around Northampton and employed over a hundred people.

From a painting Yarde's Nurseries, next to the old stone vicarage and church.

In Yarde's Tomato House, 1922, Oliver Lagden (boy) and Mr Harding, who later had a small nursery at New Duston.

Yarde and Co. name painted on the brickwork of the Abington Square premises until a few years ago.

Decorative stone carving of flowers and foliage between window bays still adorn the old Abington Square premises.

Mr Alfred Lagden Yarde's nursery manager and his son Oliver in the their garden at Duston

Oliver Lagden's wedding, 1933. Standing: Francis Mason, Ray Lagden, Oliver Lagden and Mr Marsh Seated: Clare Marsh (bride) and two bridesmaids.

Alfred Lagden's house he built for his retirement, now on the British Timken Industrial Site.

1934, Yarde's Tennis Club, included in the group are: Joan Harvey (Mrs F Golby), Ruth Harvey, Edie Toombs, Grace Blood, Silvia Hill, Phyllis Dickins, Bert Brown, Eddy Brown.

Yarde's nursery trees sale 1941 to clear ground for the first part of the factory and office site for British Timken.

R101 airship over Duston Church and Yardes Nurseries.

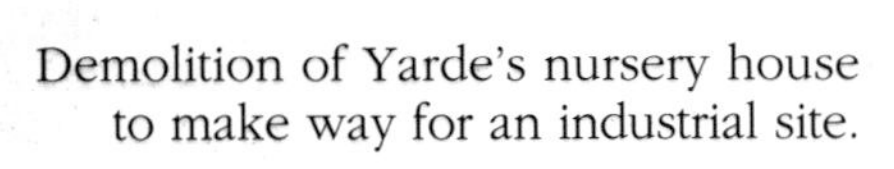

Demolition of Yarde's nursery house to make way for an industrial site.

From a painting of Yarde's nursery house off Duston Road.

Chapter 12 – Millway Nurseries and Old Mill Lane Nurseries

Bert Farmer photographed in Mill Lane Nurseries, 1922, soon after he emigrated to Canada, born in Old Duston.

Mill Lane Nurseries, 1926.

1930, bread and cheese time, dinner time at Mill Lane nurseries, men often sheltered from the wind outdoors. Cold tea from the bottle, often no milk or sugar, the top of a cottage loaf, cheese and an onion, served a long working day.

1947, Rosemary in the tulip field, Mill Way.

Takeing Geranium cuttings, Mrs Brown, 1953.

Mill Way Nurseries cold frame yards, 1961.

Chapter 13 – New Duston Stone

New Duston milestone once stood at the end of the Parish Boundary at Brook Cottage, New Duston.

Port Road quarry workers houses dating from 1840.

Good examples of Duston Stone all along Main Road, Kislingbury.

Stone Masons working in Duston's quarries, church yards in this area show the artistry of these stone masons, their intricate work on the old headstones are shown in this photograph, Mr Burt (Harpole), Mr Bowler, Mr Elliot, Mr Tom Tarry are included in the photograph.

Deep stone pits in Port Road, now all part of housing estate.

Decorative stone work on the porch of Samuel Goldbys old house in Port Road, New Duston.

Mr Dobbs large stone house (demolished for further housing) stood near Brook Cottage, New Duston.

Brook Cottage stood in former slate and stone quarry, now demolished for further housing.

All Saints Church Tower, Northampton, refurbished with Duston stone around 1935 by Henry Martin.

Quarry Road, New Duston, 1926. Quarrymans house of Mr Blunston, his stone pits extended to the site of Orchard Cottages and Harlestone Road.

Chapter 14 – Sir Robert Fossetts' Circus

Sir Robert Fossetts' Circus –
Fossetts' Circus was part of the New Duston scene at Hopping Hill for over 60 years. Although they always had their farm at Tiffield for training horses. Within the large compound at New Duston the winter months were a busy time feeding the performing elephants, lions, tigers etc. The site is now being developed for housing.

The Old Hopping Hill farm buildings, used for housing the Elephants at Fossetts' circus.

Elephant rides in the village for the children, 1926.

Old horse tram remained in old Fossetts' circus, Duston some20 years ago.

A row of disused milk carts were bought by Mr Fossett many years ago for converting into use at the circus.

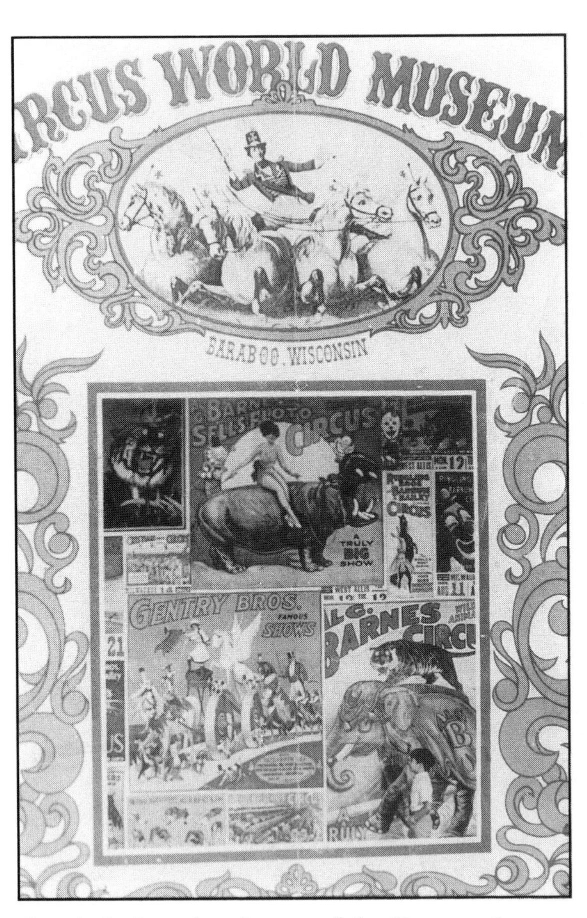

Shortly before the closure of the Duston circus site, many priceless and beautifully decorated personal living vans of generations of Fossett families were moved to a huge preservation centre for old circus travelling vans in America.

One of the beautiful gaily painted Fossett vans to be seen in this world-wide collection in America.

A day out among the travelling vans at the Massachusetts museum.
(Photos reproduced by king permission of Circus World Museum, Wisconsin, USA).

The Circus World Museum in Baraboo, Wisconsin, USA, possesses the world's largest collection of circus wagons. (Fossett)

Circus World Museum brings circus history to life with a host of entertaining and educational attractions.

Chapter 15 – New Duston

New Duston Mission, built as a daughter church to St Luke's Church, Duston in 1889 to serve the hamlet of New Duston, then most of it's labour force worked in the stone pits.

New Duston –
Duston Guide Headquarters in Port Road, 1976, this wooden building was given by British Timken, in the background is the old Duston Mission Church, afterwards named St. Barnabas, now demolished.

"Rifle Butt", 1890, the original public house had very large gardens, these areas are now used for car parks.

Opposite the Rifle Butt, 1965, fruit and vegetable shop that was once the house of Mr Blunston, quarry owner.

1946, Wegg's Farm from a painting.

Weggs Farm (now Weggs Farm Estate) was last farmed by Mr Dick Coleman who now lives in Port Road.

Watkin House when built was said to be one the finest private brickhouses in the county, built of his own bricks from the Watkin Brothers large New Duston Brickyard, the works covered most of the Hopping Hill area, it closed in 1919, Airflow Steamlines garages are now on the old workings area. This large house is now Hopping Hill Hotel.

"Quarry Arms" quarry workers public house (now Post Office).

Mr Mabbot lived in his tiny cottage in Port Road showing his prized horse at Dallington Show, 1898.

Duston baker and fish man in Port Road, 1880.

Assisting the ladies at the Victory Day cetebrations, 1945, outside New Duston Co-op (near Eldean School) Frank Neighbour, Fred Perret and Arthur Pearson.

1910. New Duston Quoits Team in the "Rifle Butt" yard, this game was also played in Melbourne Public House yard. This sport was extremely popular around the turn of the century.

1949, New Duston Primary School, Port Road (closed after the opening of Eldean School).
Included in this photo are:
1st row left to right: Sherley Slinn,, Valerie Westley, Tony George, Jean Lines, Peter Ashby, Diane Hawgood, Collin Grey, Selia Skitt, Rodney Lewin, Beryl Thompson, David Husbands, Sally Revell.
2nd row: John Spencer, Judith Penn, Martin Coleman, Maureen Faulkner, Barry Rednall, Gerald Meeton, John Husbands, Carole Perrett, Robin Loydell, John |Speight, Sheila Atkinson, Anthony Smith, Joyce Blundell.
3rd row: Margaret Garrett, Angela Robinson, Jennifer Pearson, Brenda Higinbottom, Tony Pettett, Martin Webster, Maurice Robinson, Patrick Hinsley, Stewart Pearson, Gillian Rogers, ~Susan Grey, Janice Haynes, Miss K O'Connor.
4th row: Miss K. Kilburn, Doreen Bridge, Ann Thompson, George Hawkesworth, John Ashby.
Back row: Terry Brown, Joseph Hawkesworth, Barry Smith, Ernie Johnson.

1914. Ladies of New Duston Mission Church (later St Baranabas).

New Duston Football Team in the "Rifle Butt" garden, 1914, included Mr Newbury (trainer), Mr Charlie Pendred (chairman).

Chapter 16 – Franklins Gardens

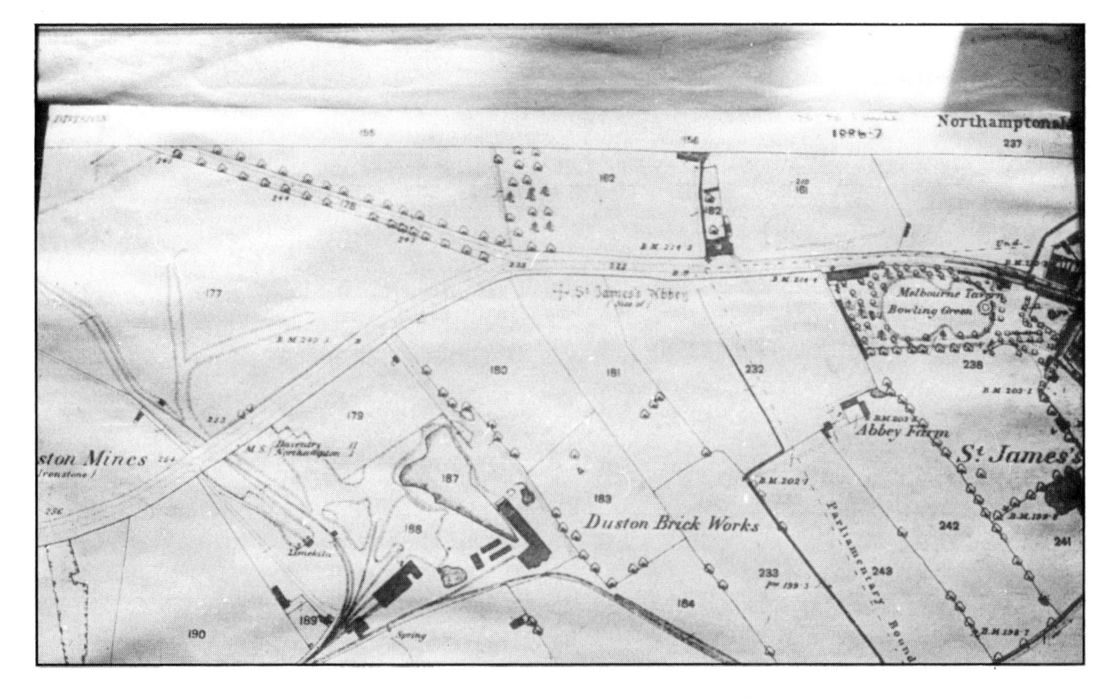

1886 map showing iron ore workings and Melbourne Gardens (later Franklins Gardens)

Calendar for 1888.

JANUARY.

S	M	T	W	T	F	S
1	2	3	4	5	6	7
8	9	10	11	12	13	14
15	16	17	18	19	20	21
22	23	24	25	26	27	28
29	30	31	...	...	...	...
...	...	...	...	...	...	...

FEBRUARY.

S	M	T	W	T	F	S
...	...	...	1	2	3	4
5	6	7	8	9	10	11
12	13	14	15	16	17	18
19	20	21	22	23	24	25
26	27	28	29	...	...	...
...	...	...	...	...	...	...

MARCH.

S	M	T	W	T	F	S
...	...	...	...	1	2	3
4	5	6	7	8	9	10
11	12	13	14	15	16	17
18	19	20	21	22	23	24
25	26	27	28	29	30	31
...	...	...	...	...	...	...

APRIL.

S	M	T	W	T	F	S
1	2	3	4	5	6	7
8	9	10	11	12	13	14
15	16	17	18	19	20	21
22	23	24	25	26	27	28
29	30	...	...	...	...	...
...	...	...	...	...	...	...

MAY.

S	M	T	W	T	F	S
...	...	1	2	3	4	5
6	7	8	9	10	11	12
13	14	15	16	17	[illegible]	19
20	21	22	23	[illegible]	25	26
27	28	29	[illegible]	[illegible]	...	...
...	...	...	...	...	...	...

JUNE.

S	M	T	W	T	F	S
...	...	...	...	...	1	2
3	4	5	6	7	8	9
10	11	12	13	14	15	16
17	18	19	20	21	22	23
24	25	26	27	28	29	30
...	...	...	...	...	...	...

JULY.

S	M	T	W	T	F	S
1	2	3	4	5	6	7
8	9	10	11	12	13	14
15	16	17	18	19	20	21
22	23	24	25	26	27	28
29	30	31	...	...	...	...
...	...	...	...	...	...	...

AUGUST.

S	M	T	W	T	F	S
...	...	...	1	2	3	4
5	6	7	8	9	10	11
12	13	14	15	16	17	18
19	20	21	22	23	24	25
26	27	28	29	30	31	...
...	...	...	...	...	...	...

SEPTEMBER.

S	M	T	W	T	F	S
...	...	...	...	...	...	1
2	3	4	5	6	7	8
9	10	11	12	13	14	15
16	17	18	19	20	21	22
23	24	25	26	27	28	29
30	...	...	...	...	...	...

OCTOBER.

S	M	T	W	T	F	S
...	1	2	3	4	5	6
7	8	9	10	11	12	13
14	15	16	17	18	19	20
21	22	23	24	25	26	27
28	29	30	31	...	...	...
...	...	...	...	...	...	...

NOVEMBER.

S	M	T	W	T	F	S
...	...	...	...	1	2	3
4	5	6	7	8	9	10
11	12	13	14	15	16	17
18	19	20	21	22	23	24
25	26	27	28	29	30	...
...	...	...	...	...	...	...

DECEMBER.

S	M	T	W	T	F	S
...	...	...	...	...	...	1
2	3	4	5	6	7	8
9	10	11	12	13	14	15
16	17	18	19	20	21	22
23	24	25	26	27	28	29
30	31	...	...	...	...	...

FRANKLIN'S HOTEL,

(Two Doors from the New Opera House, which is open every evening.)

GUILDHALL ROAD, NORTHAMPTON,

DINNERS IN THE PUBLIC DINING ROOM

From 12 to 3, at Moderate Charges.

Luncheons, Wedding Breakfasts, Ball Suppers, &c., supplied by Contract.

Plate, Linen, Glass and Table Decorations on Hire.

N.B.—J. C. Franklin takes this opportunity of informing his friends of his latest speculation—

THE PLEASURE GARDENS, DUSTON ROAD,

which are now replete with every convenience and accommodation for Visitors. The Grounds are open all the year round, and an ever-changing Programme of Innocent Amusement and Recreation is provided.

SEASON TICKETS 10/- EACH.

P.T.O.

Proprietor—J. C. FRANKLIN.

Mr Franklin's calendar of 1888.

Mr Franklins reverse side of calendar.

Old gardener's houses, Franklin's Gardens. The gable ends are built of bricks built in alternative courses of ribbed moulding containing holes through which wire could be passed horizontally to provide an ideal framework f or climbing and ornamental plants.

Gardener's houses showing "Melbourne Place" stone plaque, the yew tree is said to be the same age as the the buildings.

The remains of old Franklin's Gardens Café still to be seen in the now large car park.

Old Franklin's Gardens Hotel, demolished in the 1930s to widen Weedon Road.

1952. Salon-de-Dance old band stand bedecked with floral decoration for an important occasion.

Salon-de-Dance, Franklin's Gardens, in 1920s, it's west front and entrance adorned with plants and flowers.

The water area south of the gardens originally laid out as an ornamental lake for boating etc.

These extensive tennis courts were once part of the large sportng activities at Franklin's Gardens.

This pavilion and it's well kept greens were part of West End Bowling Club fot over 50 years before they moved to Old Duston.

Swiss Cottage, this lovely old thatched building was once part of Franklin's Gardens.

Chapter 17 – St James Abbey

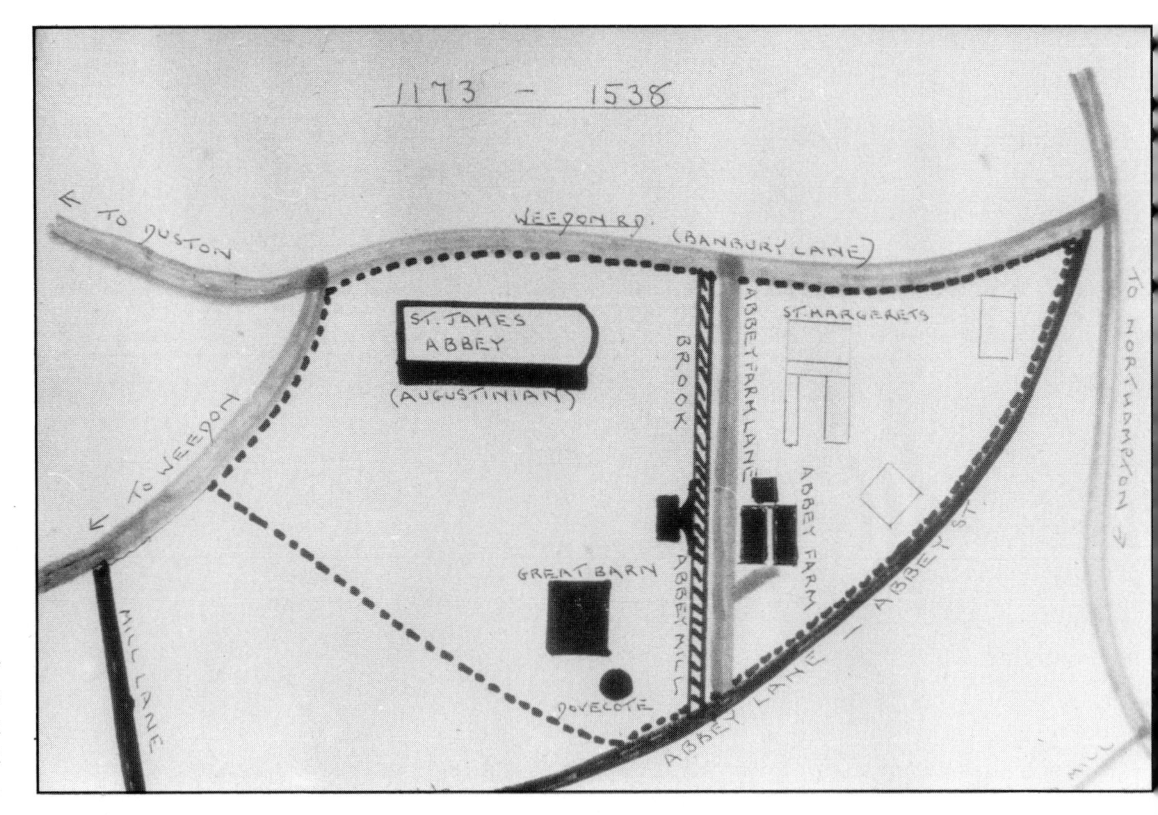

Plan of 12th century site of St James Abbey from Weedon Road south to St James Square.

Tomb cover of the thirteenth Abbot of St James Abbey in St Luke's Church, Duston, it is assumed that the monks of St James Abbey built the early part of this church and after the dissolution of the Abbey much of it's sandstone was reused for the 16th century additions to the church. The Abbey stood only a few fields away from the church for some 400 years.

St James Abbey boundary wall which remained 150 years ago from Melbourne Road to the top of Weedon Road, a short length in front of Abbey Works still remains.

Misericord tip up oak chancel seats taken from St James Abbey after the dissolution of the monastery in 1538 and placed in Gayton Church.

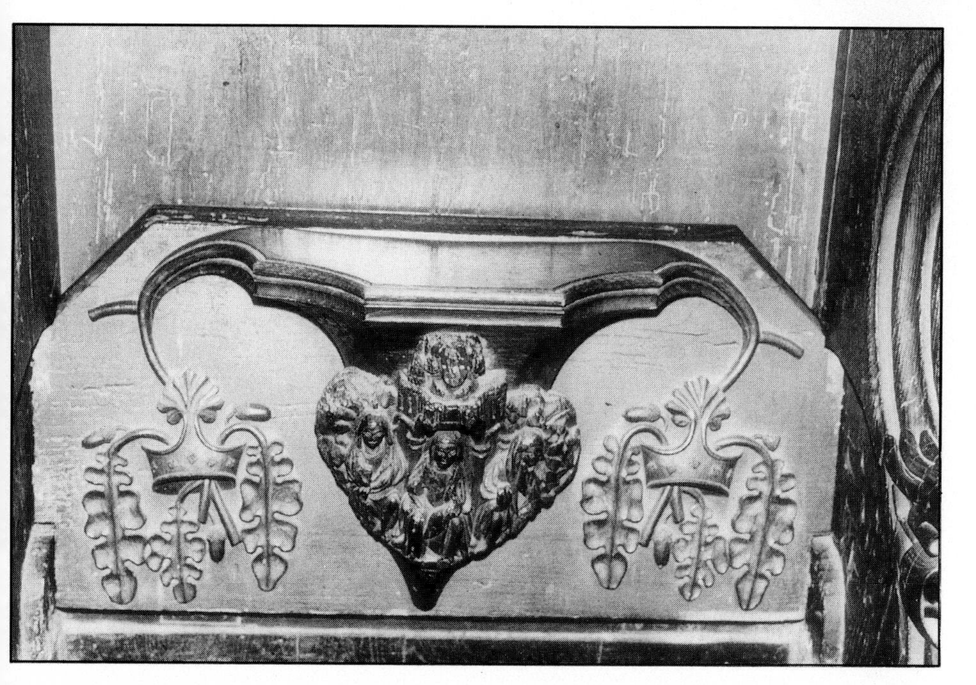

Each of these six seats depict scenes from the bible when lifted up in their upright position.

Chapter 18 – St James

1950. Aerial photograph showing Whitton's "last" works, St James cinema ("Roxy". In the foreground). Left "Robin Hood", "The Old Tin Shop". Opposite the entrance to the Old Cedos Works.

"Duston Villa" stood in St James Road opposite Argyle Street and was the home of Robert Whitton 'The Last Man" he built his large factory in St James Road in 1905. His son Robert still owns these manufacturing premises.

The old paper shop, St James Road, first Mr Walter Handley, then his son kept it going for fifty years.

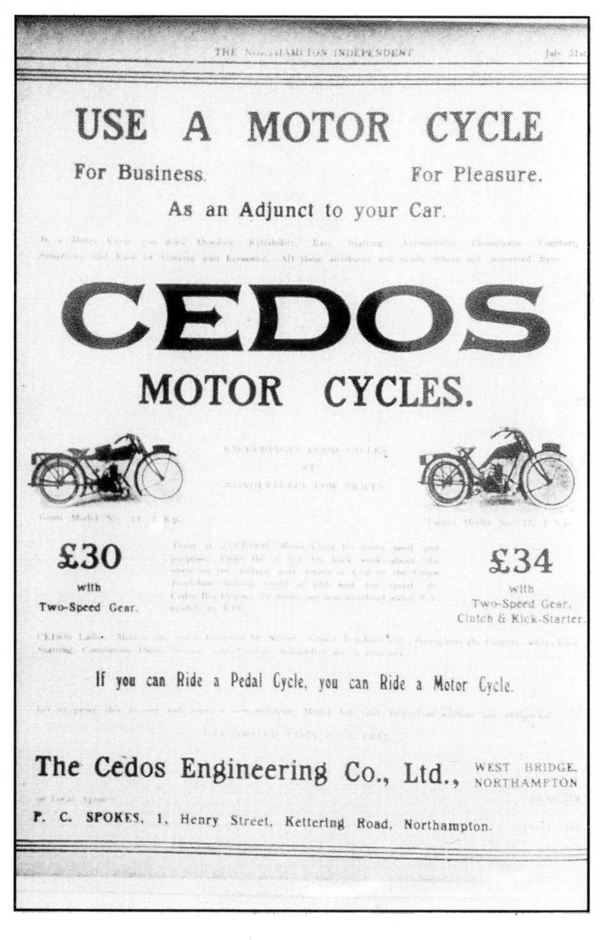

From catatogue of Cedos Engineering Co. of their Westbridge Works, by 1926 a new company "Cedos Motorcycles" moved to Brunswick Place where production ended in 1927. Various Cedos Companies operated at Westbridge from that date.

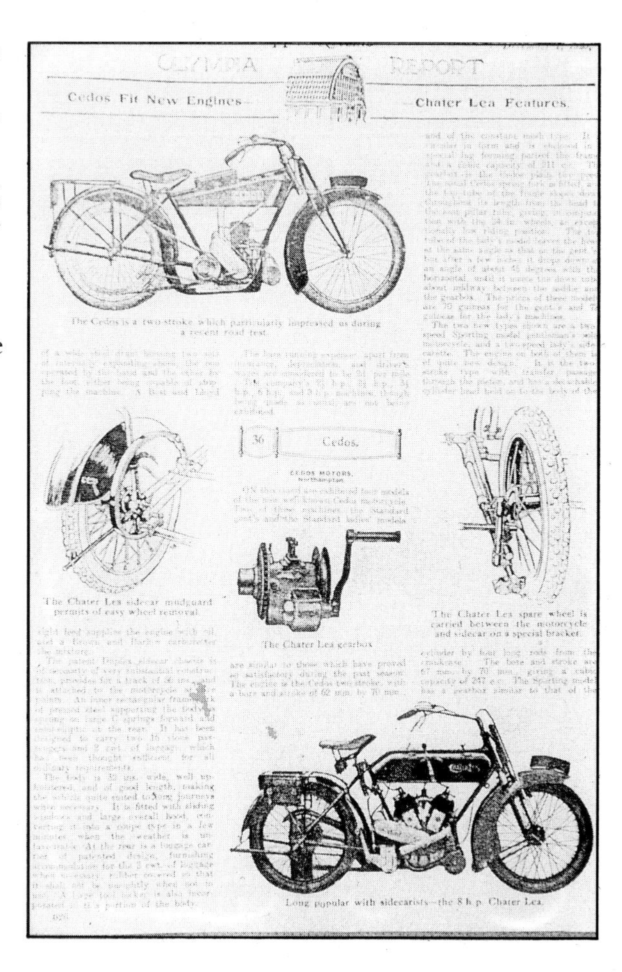

OLYMPIA REPORT

Cedos Fit New Engines — Chater Lea Features.

The Cedos is a two-stroke which particularly impressed us during a recent road test.

36 Cedos.

CEDOS MOTORS, Northampton.

The Chater Lea sidecar mudguard permits of easy wheel removal.

The Chater Lea gearbox

The Chater Lea spare wheel is carried between the motorcycle and sidecar on a special bracket.

Long popular with sidecarists—the 8 h.p. Chater Lea.

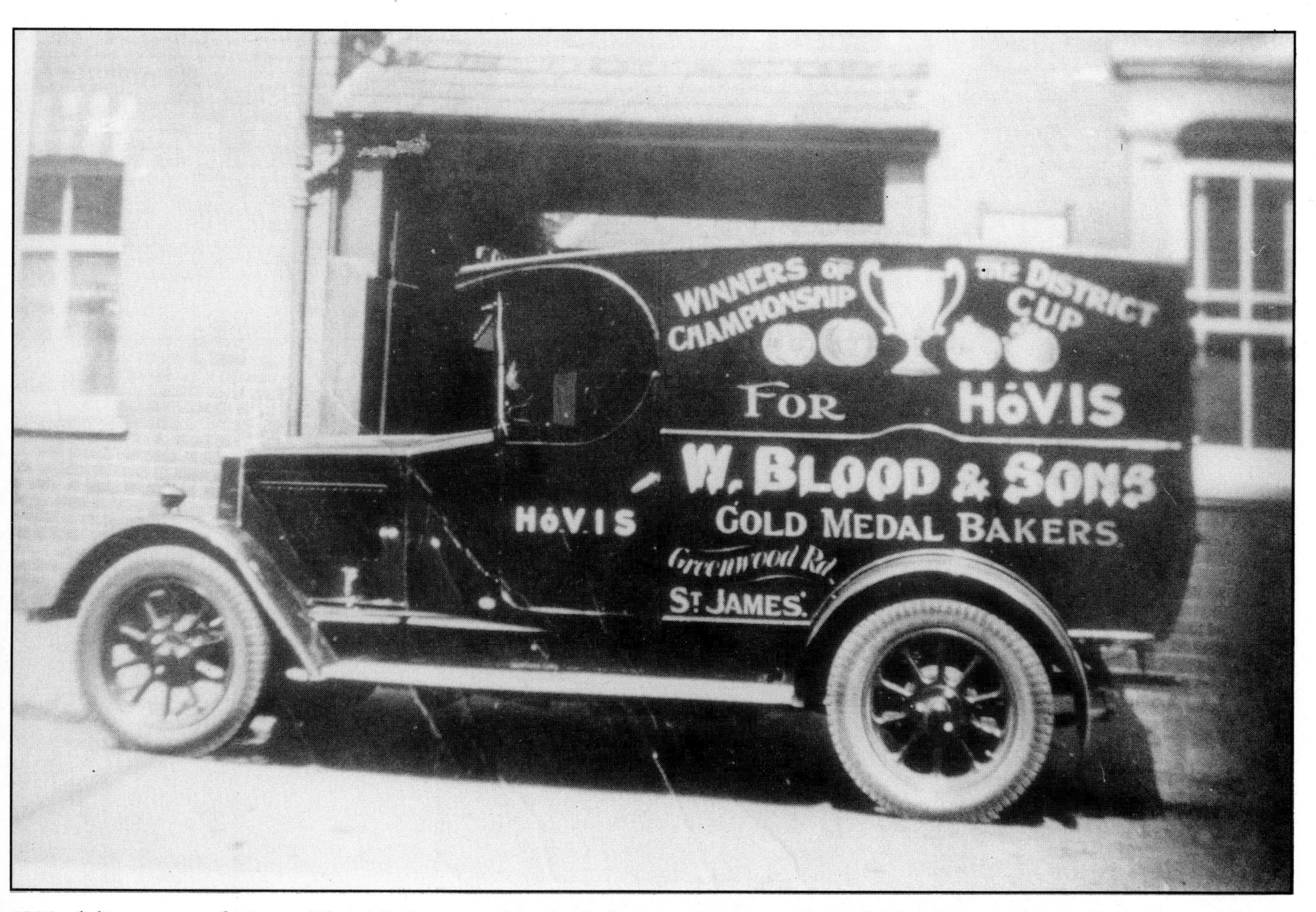

1928, delivery van of Messrs Blood & Sons outside the bakery in Greenwood Road. Their National awards were proudly shown on the van.

Before demolishing for road widening, this collection of old retail shops serviced this old part of St James End.

Outdoor beer house and general grocery of Mr Slinn, St James Park Road, this was a heavily populated area with its sorrounding streets including Park Wood Street, built for railway workers, a large part of the area is now demolished.

Brown's Corn Shop, Harlestone Road, the family ran this Pet and Seed Shop for over 50 years, atthough this property now stands empty it is now probably one of the last Duston Stone properties still standing in St James.

Doddridge Memorial Boy's Brigade Sunday Parade in St. James Main road 1939. Brimleys wireless shop in the background.

1877, this first small building in Sandhill Road was the beginning of Primitive Methodist worship in St James, later the imposing building on tbe corner of Sandhill Road and Har1estone Road was erected, a complete new modern church has now been built at Harlestone Road, New Duston.

Datestone of the first primitive Methodist Chapel in Sandhill Road, St James.

1865 Doddridge Memorial's Sunday School was built and later demolished to make way for much larger premises.

Mr Amos, headmaster St James Church of England School, retired 1924.

1936, Pantomime at Orbiston School for girls, Holrood Road, St. James. After the last war the school moved to Upton Hall and the name of the school was eventually changed to Quinton House School.

Alma Street, St James, 1936, King George's Silver Jubilee, when everybody's dining table came out and was placed end to end down the street, each street in St James seemed to be overflowing with children then.

Northampton Pageant in Abington Park, 1925. A photograph presented to Mrs L L Price showing the "St James Episode" among those who took part, Eric James, Stafford Garnett, Reverend Harold Bickley,

1928, Pageant Abington Park. Back row: 2. Florrie Harris Woodland, 3. Barbara Waddington, 4. Mollie Tomalin, 7. Bernard Brown, 10. Rev Bickley, 11. Stafford Garnett, 17. Mrs. Sear, 18. Stella Soal. Front row: 4 Margaret Mackness, 5. Molly Mackness, 6. Phyllis Drage, 8. Eric James, 10. Mable Wilson, 11, Louise Merry, 12. Nellie Pettifer.

Westbridge Motors, 1938, in the background can be seen the old granary and the projecting housing for the lifting gear to unload grain from barges which used the narrow waterways adjacent to the Nene yeas ago.

Dodderidge Memorial 4th company and Castle Hill 1st company Boy's Brigade combined camp at Gorleston 1947. Officers seated: Lt. R Harris, Lt. E. Jeyes, Cpt. Farey, Lt. Shadwell, The Rev. Coxon, Lt. W. Wright, Lt. W. Mallard, Lt. E. Goine, Lt. E. Bentley, Lt. S. Attwood.

Cafe Square, 1898, note tram lines were for early horse drawn trams.

St James Square before the first war, on the left Mill's Dairy and Mr Strike's greengrocers shop with sun blinds.

The Old Toll House, St James Square, (later police station, finally Pells shop).

St James Church newly built in 1868 in Early English Style in brick, an oak channel screen was added in 1920, since the extensive interior alterations a few years ago it has been removed to the west end of the church.

1926, St James Church Choir of over 40 members, taken in the church garden and with the Girls School Buildings in the background.

Doddridge Memorial RFC 1928

Front row, left to right: C W Lewis, J L Price (Hon. Sec.), W Coombes, D Draper, W Gotch (Captn), A Plackett, W Winkworth, A E Shadwell.
Back row, left to right: L Brown, J Colins (Hon. Tres.), F Merriman, J J Ruddick, V Radford, H Radford, F Hoar, G A Hewitt, A E Carter, J Montgomery, F W Miller, H Perkins.

ISBN 0-9518569-0-1
9 780951 856901
00699

GREATEST TRACTORS

Fordson Icons

- Fordson F to Super Major
- Owners' collections
- Restorations
- Buyer's guides